The Circle of Enduring Love

The Circle of Enduring Love

A Celebration of Romance and Affection

PAT ROSS

Andrews McMeel Publishing

Kansas City

www.andrewsmcmeel.com
98 99 00 01 TWP 10 9 8 7 6 5 4 3 2 1

Set in Sabon
Designed by Virginia Norey

LIBRARY OF CONGRESS CATALOGING-IN-PUBLICATION DATA

Ross, Pat, 1943-
    The circle of enduring love : a celebration of romance and affection / Pat Ross.
        p.   cm.
    ISBN 0-8362-6965-9 (hardcover : alk. paper)
    1. Love--Quotations, maxims, etc.   I. Title.
PN6084.L6R67 1998   98-7798
808.88'2--dc21   CIP

ATTENTION: SCHOOLS AND BUSINESSES
Andrews McMeel books are available at quantity discounts
with bulk purchase for educational, business, or sales promotional use.
For information, please write to:
Special Sales Department,
Andrews McMeel Publishing,
4520 Main Street, Kansas City, Missouri 64111.

For my sister
Jeanne Kienzle

❧

who mends broken hearts

Jeanne Kienzle Wartenberg
with Gerd Wartenberg.

Preface

A romantic at heart, I can remember the very first time a boy kissed me in earnest, and the way his father's cologne was tinged with acne lotion. The experience filled me with mixed emotions, and I was never quite the same again. It's easy for most of us to probe deeply into cherished memories and come up with the full names and quirky expressions of old flames, the intoxicating fragrance of a prom corsage, or the exact texture of a partner's hair. Four years ago, I fell irreversibly in love with a gentle man who waded knee-deep into a weedy ravine along a solitary country road to pick black-eyed Susans and Queen Anne's lace for me. It seems this changed my point of view both personally and professionally, because my passion for collecting old photographs took a coincidental turn in content.

I suddenly found myself drawn to images of romantic couples—men and women of all ages—captured in moments that seemed to express their powerful emotions in just one glance. Previously, I had thought the truly great and spontaneous photographs of lovers were mostly famous and mostly French. But then, much like suddenly finding four-leaf clovers on every hillside, I came across delightful images at my usual haunts—antique shops, ephemera shows, and local flea markets. Here were piles and boxes of photographs to sort through, looking for the gems.

Until our recent past, holding hands in public and other more overt romantic gestures were thought inappropriate. So often, lovers held broad smiles and shy poses for the camera. Occasionally, however, they'd be caught off guard, kissing or teasing playfully, or in even more touching unrehearsed poses. The more formal wedding portraits of the past, printed on fine heavy stock, reflected the importance of this special day, and that has not changed. It hardly mattered that the lovers in the photos that I found were anonymous, for I quickly fell for them all. Finally, when I surveyed my growing collection, I knew I had to compile a book—this book.

To supplement my collection I wrote to friends, who ended up thanking *me* for asking them to search through their long-neglected photo albums. As usual, my own family of photograph hounds got into the act, and I wound up with several memorable images that I'm certain I would have selected myself. Little by little, the ages and stages of love emerged, fresh, recognizable, and endearing.

When I had assembled a group of photographs, I enlisted Leisa Crane—a friend, a perceptive researcher, and a hopeless romantic, too—to help me search for authors who had written insightfully and wittily of romantic attachments. The matches that resulted were as heady as first love.

Then came the daunting task of writing an introduction. What qualifications did I possess to take on a subject that I knew only from a limited and personal perspective? Like most of us, I had bungled love more than once; this time around, it seemed that I was getting it right. But did that qualify me to *discuss* love? When the time came to write a few pages for this introduction, I froze. Then I remembered that I had an expert on the subject of love right in my family. If anyone could make some sense of the vicissitudes

of romantic love, it would be my sister, Jeanne Kienzle! I knew that Jeanne, an experienced psychotherapist who works exclusively with couples, could come up with some fitting thoughts. Whenever I'm stuck in some emotional quagmire, I make a transatlantic phone call for a session with my sister (who, unfortunately, lives in Germany). My phone and fax bills are outrageous, but, as Jayne Anne Phillips writes: "Talk between friends is always therapy."

Soon Jeanne began faxing back her ideas about romantic love. Suddenly, a subject that was previously rather confusing to me began to have a pattern, a flow, a profile. A spirited commentary began to emerge. And so I have included my sister's thoughts as the introduction to *The Circle of Enduring Love*. She succeeded in conveying to me in an organized and revealing way what most of us have either experienced firsthand, suspected, or simply wondered about. I am thrilled and comforted that love is possible for all of us at any age or stage of our lives.

Introduction

Jeanne Kienzle

Romantic themes in all forms of art have a way of capturing the hearts of even the least sentimental audiences. Most people can identify with the plight of lovers even if their own personal experience of romantic love has been confined to one precious, brief moment—or they haven't yet encountered that moment. Surely, it is a rare event for two people to fall in love with each other, and most mysterious of all is the gift of romantic love that abides and deepens between lovers over many years together. While there are no magic formulas to guarantee enduring love, there are some patterns that lead to sustained caring and endearment.

A journey into romantic love begins when, quite unexpectedly, we find ourselves extending our limits to embrace the "otherness" of a beloved. Our actions swell with unusual generosity, and with each gesture we are open to everything new and wonderfully strange. Before the moment of romantic awakening, there may have been a dull awareness of something "missing." And then an "a-ha" experience takes place. Often there is a sudden, overwhelming feeling of loneliness and shallowness of life. We realize we need to be valued for our particular feelings and views. We wish for someone else to balance our one-sidedness by providing all those qualities we have been lacking. What becomes most clear is a deep longing for the comforting presence of a soul mate to share private thoughts and outer interests, someone who appreciates and understands us like no other. Feelings of independence are expanded to feelings of "we" and "us," and then further extended to a sense of belonging together in the world as a union of positive energies. For those who haven't had special creative or spiritual moments in their lives, romantic love—a possibility for everyone—may be the first time they experience the thrill of going beyond the mundane limits of their existence.

"Falling in love" has been likened to the sudden onset of insanity—one's previous world turned upside down. It is a fall from any logical, sensible, predictable, or commonly validated reality. Before the plunge there is a flash of recognition that "this could be heaven or this could be hell," but then it is already too late. The realm of reason is lost as the soul is swept away on a magic carpet ride, or plummeted into a seething cauldron of desires. Others around may remark, "He's head over heels in love with her," or "She's absolutely nuts about him." But their comments are superfluous, because the one in love is in the grip of a compelling wish to be with the beloved.

Just as in certain forms of madness, people describe falling in love as if they are possessed by a powerful force that overwhelms their senses and robs them of choice. They may behave in ways that appear wildly erratic, inexplicably withdrawn, or embarrassingly foolish. They may abandon caring families and lucrative jobs, skip meals, and ignore oncoming traffic while crossing the street. Acts of boasting or exaggeration may complete a picture of just plain craziness that looks so silly it draws laughter or ridicule. Nevertheless, there is something enviable and irresistible about this odd state. Although falling in love is the most radical loss of equilibrium a person can sustain—next to genuine insanity the excitement of the "fall" can be an inspiration to dissolve outworn, rigid attitudes and transform them into creative impulses.

Without idealizing another person, probably no one would ever fall in love or stay in love. Idealization makes lasting love possible by letting us selectively see the most fascinating, admirable, creative resources the beloved offers. The perfect inner core of the other person is what the lover first sees. In films of the Wild West, this idealization has been stereotyped as "the heart of gold beneath the rough exterior." The lovers have uncanny insight into each other's very best potential, no matter how they may appear on the surface.

Idealizing the beloved makes it easy to overlook even obvious shortcomings and undesirable habits. Shakespeare wrote, "My mistress's eyes are nothing like the sun . . ." Crooked teeth, a disorderly desk, and even poor taste or unpredictability seem irrelevant, considering the bliss provided by the more delightful qualities of the beloved. When intuition has been trustworthy and admiration withstands the test of time, idealization gradually becomes modified by a more realistic view of the beloved. New interest is aroused by the continuing mystery of differing gifts.

The transition from infatuation to a more enduring romantic love involves a gradual widening of horizons. At first, the lovers are exclusively concerned with each other. It's difficult to hear what others are saying, to remember appointments, or be interested in political crises, because thoughts of the beloved are all-consuming. Before each reunion, they reminisce about their earlier glorious moments together, and, afterward, spend time in joyful anticipation of the next meeting. Truly, lovers only have eyes for each other. When they've reached more intimate acquaintance with each others' minds and bodies, then the world may be allowed back into the relationship. But now it is a world alive with rich details never before registered with such intensity. A sunset enjoyed together fills life with new meaning and the quickened awareness of time.

The lovers begin to play with possibilities for the future and sketch out

ideas for fulfilling their dreams. Designing a garden, selecting a vacation spot, or organizing a party to celebrate the new partnership may be part of this process. For some couples, selecting rings symbolizes their union in a traditional way. Less conventional couples may choose to get married flying high above the ground in a colorful hot-air balloon or poised in a field of daisies. In any case, it is usually some ritual or symbol that ushers in the plan of how to build a life together.

Fairy tales describe how lovers overcome a series of obstacles to eventual union. But they don't tell us how to live happily ever after! The challenge of keeping a romance alive often exhausts the lovers' creative resources and defies their best intentions as they enter the middle years of work and family responsibilities. Yet we look with wonder upon those couples who "hold it together" for life. Juggling the stress of children's needs, competitive jobs, demanding in-laws, and boring housework, some people are still thrilled to receive red roses from their partner. Others experience the spontaneous urge to whisper "I love you," just to see their lover's eyes brighten with pleasure.

The key to this treasure seems to be an inner resolution to take *time* for love, *whether or not* the outer shuffle of duties and appointments allows for that time together. Enduring love is nurtured only if some special time is reserved—just for the lovers alone—in which playfulness and lightheartedness emerge without effort. Then they listen to each other's needs and renew the original enchantment that brought them together.

Another aspect of keeping the vitality in a lifelong affair of the heart is the individual freedom that forms the basis of genuine attachment. The lovers respect each other's separate identities and avoid a smothering "togetherness." Even after many years of familiarity, partners still find each other charming if there is some facet that's mysterious, elusive, or not entirely predictable. At the same time, lovers need to develop an unquestionable level of trust and reliability. Undoubtedly, it is an ongoing quest to find the

right balance between closeness and distance in loving, but continuing the interplay of these opposites seems to hold couples together.

When we have become deeply involved with a partner, one fact becomes painfully clear: This love implies an enormous risk! When our lover is absent, we may have everything we need to be happy and self-sufficient, and yet there is a gnawing feeling of "missing" that special person. For the beloved to be gone forever would be an unbearable loss. But the price of enduring love is exactly that insight.

In the autumn of life, enduring love may reach its finest expression. Doubts about achievement, worries over material security, and the routine of old roles fade into the background, while issues of meaning, refinement of interests, and concern for others come to the fore.

Most individuals have suffered some failures in love relationships.

Resentment, jealousy, and ambivalence may have ruined promising partnerships. But by this time many people look forward to a "second (or third) time around," one with greater compassion than in the past. A few couples may have weathered all the storms and are ready for a change of pace together—this time with fewer duties, more passion, and more fun.

At this stage, romantic love may show some parallels with an earlier phase of "falling in love." Couples may express "pure foolishness" by making plans and carrying out projects that would have seemed exotic or impractical in the child-rearing years. There is the chance to travel, to flee to more stimulating terrain, or to live out a dream never realized but never abandoned. All these possibilities, of course, provide new ways for the lovers to show each other their talents with spontaneity and confidence. Being proud of the beloved seems to belong most to the "autumn" years.

It seems unjust that the *expression* of deep appreciation and gratitude between lovers is often reserved for the later part of life. Apparently, it takes a long time for most people to grasp that a loving partnership is the product of willing engagement and untiring effort, as much as it is a gift of grace.

The lovers who have won each other's hearts and achieved some form of lasting endearment all share one very important survival skill. They have learned to laugh together. In the final analysis, the capacity to see the strange and comic sides in each other renews the fascination of love. It is a sense of humor that completes the circle of enduring love.

PART ONE

Girl Meets Boy

First love is an astounding experience and if the object happens to be totally unworthy and love not really love at all, it makes little difference to the intensity of the pain.

—Angela Thirkell,
1941

*M*any a man has kissed a girl whom he had not the least desire to kiss, just because that was easier than trying to think up something to say to her.

—Helen Rowland,
1927

I am like a falling star who has finally found her place next to another in a lovely constellation, where we will sparkle in the heavens forever.

—Amy Tan,
1995

Patsy Kienzle, Queen of the May, with her king in 1948.

I *abhor the slimy kiss,*

    (Which to me most loathsome is.)

Those lips please me which are placed

Close, but not too strictly laced:

Yielding I would have them; yet

Not a wimbling Tongue admit:

What should poking-sticks make there,

When the ruffle is set elsewhere?

               —Robert Herrick,
                   1648

And stretching out his arm he pressed it about her waist. The attempt she made to disengage herself was only feeble. He continued to support her as they walked.

—Gustave Flaubert,
1857

*T*he sound of a kiss is not so loud as that of a cannon, but its echo lasts a great deal longer.

—Oliver Wendell Holmes,
1860

*O*ne of the more serious worries that besets a newly married man is his wife's girl friend. . . . The girl friend said good-bye to the bride immediately after the ceremony all right, but as soon as the honeymoon was over she appeared, bright-eyed and eager, on the doormat if not, indeed, at the railroad station when the train came in.

—Emily Hahn,
1956

Lenore "Leni" Goldman and Bob Simon picnicking with friends in Van Cortland Park, the Bronx, around 1949, "before we tied the knot."

"*Because*," *he said*, "I sometimes have a queer feeling with regard to you—especially when you are near me, as now: it is as if I had a string somewhere under my left ribs, tightly and inextricably knotted to a similar string situated in the corresponding quarter of your little frame."

—Charlotte Brontë,
1847

$\mathcal{L}$*ove me* in full being.

—Elizabeth Barrett Browning
(1806–1861)

John and Mary Louise Clark exploring remote
and romantic Cedar Island, Virginia.

You are the very one I've searched for
In many lands in every weather.
You are my sort; you understand me;
As equals we can talk together.

— Heinrich Heine
(1797–1856)

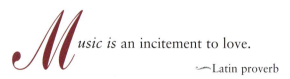 *M*usic *is* an incitement to love.

~Latin proverb

Jitterbugging at a juke joint, Mississippi, 1939

*Audrey Strachan and a beau traveling
somewhere in Europe in the 1930s.*

Let us be frank. The bathing beach affords many a glimpse of pulchritude. What better may reveal a pretty curve than wind and wave?

—Paul McPharlin,
1946

I *was not merely* over head and heels in
love with her, but I was saturated
through and through.

⸺Charles Dickens,
1850

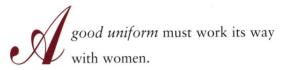

A good uniform must work its way with women.

⟶Charles Dickens, 1837

We sat in the car park until twenty to one
And now I'm engaged to Miss Joan Hunter Dunn.

— Sir John Betjeman,
1945

*I*t is then that a strange desperation grips the youths and young girls walking up and down and meeting at regular intervals. Each man transcends himself, becomes handsome and irresistible like a Don Juan, and his eyes express a murderous strength that chills a woman's heart. The girls' eyes sink deeper and reveal deep labyrinthine pools. Their pupils distend, open without resistance, and admit those conquerors who stare into their opaque darkness. . . .

—Bruno Schulz,
1977

A formal occasion at Hood College in the late 1930s.

My dear, I don't care what they do so long as they don't do it in the street and frighten the horses.

⌐Attributed to Mrs. Patrick Campbell
(1865–1940)

*N*othing is more true, more real,
   than the primeval magnetic disturbances
that two souls may communicate to one another,
through the tiny sparks of a moment's glance.

—Victor Hugo
(1802–1885)

A *tender, sensitive female* tells how she felt when first he kissed her—
like a tub of roses swimming in honey,
cologne, nutmeg and blackberries.

—Samuel Cox,
1876

Erika and Gary Matt, 1998.

If I never met him I would have dreamed him into being.

—Anzia Yezierska,
1950

It struck me then that up to now I had spent little time kissing; oh, there had been the usual connections, of course, but relatively little of the tender holding and inhaling without which love in life is a mere scamper. Swan and I spent hour upon hour with our faces close together, appointed to wear out proximity as an hypnotic device. . . . There was a gift of mutual immersion I had never known before, requiring no training and no motive, but only the sublime sink into liquid hommage.

—Paul West,
1996

PART TWO

Promises

*Love is strange bewilderment which overtakes
one person on account of another person.*
— James Thurber and E. B. White,
1929

*H*e is the greatest institution of this country.
And, believe me, there is no other country in
this world that produces such shoes, such rocking chairs,
such bathtubs, such green corn, such watermelon and
such Ideal Husbands!

—Helen Rowland,
1927

METAMORPHOSIS

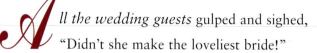*ll the wedding guests* gulped and sighed,
 "Didn't she make the loveliest bride!"

Brides in the country, brides in the city,

Brides who really are far from pretty,

Brides who are rich, and brides who are poor,

Brides who are young, and brides mature,

Brides with dimples, and brides without,

Brides too slender, and brides too stout . . .

All of the happy ones whose faces

Shine with rapture at twenty paces,

Suddenly look so ornamental,

Eyes triumphant and smiles so dental

Friends in all sincerity say,

"What a beauty she is today!"

Joy's a sorcerer, joy's a magician,

And Cupid's a practicing beautician.

—Margaret Fishback,
1938

*Jerri and Carl Fowler leaving for their Florida honeymoon from
Pennsylvania Station, Baltimore, Maryland, 1948.*

*T*raveling *together* is a great test,
which has damaged many friendships
and even honeymoons."

—Dame Rose Macaulay,
1956

A husband, like any other wedding-present, is always a surprise—and the only thing to do is try to get used to him, just as you have to get used to the blue china console set and the hand-painted parlor lamp.

—Helen Rowland,
1927

An anonymous wedding couple as portrayed in a formal portrait by Van B. Wheaton of Amsterdam, New York.

It is better to know as little as possible of the defects of the person with whom you are to pass your life.

—Jane Austen,
1813

Supposing that the parents absolutely forbid a marriage,
the young couple of course elopes if they really love each other.
This has long been considered more romantic than the usual sanctioned
procedure, and to tell the truth is much less fussy and expensive.
The father in particular escapes paying for flowers, decorations and
announcements. If the young couple fails to receive wedding presents
from scandalized aunts, so much the better for their starting in
housekeeping: they are not embarassed by gadgets they have no use for.

—Paul McPharlin,
1946

*H*e took *the bride* about the neck
And kissed her lips with such a clamorous smack
That at parting, all the church did echo.

— William Shakespeare,
1594

*I*f it is your time love will track you down
like a cruise missile. If you say "No! I don't want it
right now," that's when it will get you for sure. Love will
make a way out of no way. Love's an exploding cigar
which we willingly smoke.

—Lynda Barry,
1983

Frances and Michael Cohn on their honeymoon in 1923; photo is noted
"The Soul Kiss at Niagara Falls, September 13, 1923."

Photo taken from an early stereoscopic card from St. Louis, Missouri.

*N*ever go to bed mad.
Stay up and fight.

~~Phyllis Diller,
1966

I *am Tarzan of the Apes*. I want you. I am yours. You are mine. We will live here together always in my house. I will bring you the best fruits, the tenderest deer, the finest meats that roam the jungle. I will hunt for you. I am the greatest of the jungle hunters. I will fight for you. I am the mightiest of the jungle fighters. You are Jane Porter, I saw it in your letter. When you see this you will know that it is for you and that Tarzan of the Apes loves you.

—Edgar Rice Burroughs,
1914

A young gentleman, though he lack the customary introduction, may rescue a young lady from drowning. This may be the beginning of a long friendship, providing, of course, the young lady be not beyond resuscitation.

—Paul McPharlin,
1946

"*Oh Martin, you may be* slow spoken, but you're quick enough at some things," laughed Margie as she retreated to the window, struggling hard against the throb of reckless elation that arose in her. She felt as though some great force had been unlocked within her, great and terrible enough to rend her asunder, as when a brake snaps or a band slips and some ponderous machine grinds itself in pieces. It is not an easy thing, after a woman has shut the great natural hope out of her life, to open the flood gates and let the riotous, aching current come throbbing again through the shrunken channels, waking a thousand undreamed-of possibilities of pleasure and pain.

—Willa Cather,
1897

*W*here *you used to be,* there is a hole in the
world, which I find myself constantly walking
around in the daytime, and falling into at night.
I miss you like hell.

—Edna St. Vincent Millay
(1892–1950)

Soul meets soul on lovers' lips.
—Percy Bysshe Shelley,
1820

*Jean Jackson and Jeff Fowler on their Cancun, Mexico,
honeymoon, June 1995.*

To see coming toward you the face that will mean an end of oneness is—far more than birth itself—the beginning of life.

—Holly Roth,
1953

*P*erhaps *this is* in the end what most marriages are—gentleness, memory, and habit.

—Storm Jameson,
1932

Barclay and Aggie Rives with daughter, Caroline.

When You Are Old

When you are old and gray and full of sleep,
And nodding by the fire, take down this book,
And slowly read, and dream of the soft look
Your eyes had once, and of their shadows deep.

How many loved your moments of glad grace,
And loved your beauty with love false or true,
But one man loved the pilgrim soul in you,
And loved the sorrows of your changing face;

And bending down beside the glowing bars,
Murmur, a little sadly, how Love fled
And paced upon the mountains overhead
And hid his face amid a crowd of stars.

—William Butler Yeats,
1906

"*H*ome" is any four walls that enclose the right person.

—Helen Rowland,
1909

*T*o *love deeply* in one direction makes us
more loving in all others.

— Anne-Sophie Swetchine,
1869

MA AND PA

The logic of the heart is absurd.

～Julie de Lespinasse,
1774

*S*exiness *wears thin* after a while and beauty fades, but to be married to a man who makes you laugh every day, ah, now that's a treat.

⤙Attributed to Joanne Woodward

The photograph that Cindy and Eddie Russell (with Penny) used on their 1997 Christmas card.

PART THREE

Love Is Ageless

Young love is a flame, often very hot and fierce but still only light and flickering. The love of an older and disciplined heart is as coals deep-burning, unquenchable.

—Henry Ward Beecher
(1813–1887)

As he entered the drawing-room his heart beat violently, and his hands trembled so perceptibly that he clasped them behind his back. His first emotion was shame, as if every one in the room already knew that he had just been embraced and kissed.
He retired into his shell, and looked fearfully around. But finding that hosts and guests were calmly dancing or talking, he regained courage, and surrendered himself to sensations experienced for the first time in life. The unexampled had happened. His neck, fresh from the embrace of two soft, scented arms, seemed anointed with oil; near his left mustache, where the kiss had fallen, trembled a slight, delightful chill, as from peppermint drops; and from head to foot he was soaked in new and extraordinary sensations, which continued to grow and grow.

Anton Chekhov
(1860–1904)

*N*othing *moves a woman* so deeply as the boyhood of the man she loves.

—Annie Dillard,
1992

JENNY KISSED ME

*J*enny *kissed me* when we met,
   Jumping from the chair she sat in;
   Time, you thief, whose love to get
Sweets into your list, put that in!
Say I'm weary, say I'm sad,
Say that health and wealth have missed me,
Say I'm growing old, but add,
Jenny kissed me.

Leigh Hunt,
1844

Jennie and Clarence Hooper at their anniversary party on December 11, 1948.
Since the date was also his birthday, the family held a party every year without fail.
Clarence was buried on December 11, 1973. Jennie was adrift without her soul mate,
until she died many years later at the age of ninety-three.

The secret anniversaries of the heart.

— Henry Wadsworth Longfellow,
1876

We love because it's the only true adventure.

— Nikki Giovanni,
1976

*T*rust *in my affection* for you. Tho' I may not display it exactly in the way you like and expect it, it is not therefore less deep and sincere.

—Anna Jameson,
1833

Note jotted in pencil on the back of this small snapshot says: This is myself and Hub and Brother Ed and Wife. She looks so sober and she is not that way at all.

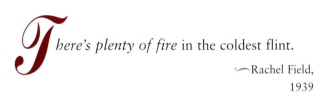

*T*here's *plenty of fire* in the coldest flint.

— Rachel Field,
1939

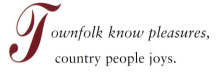

Townfolk know pleasures,
country people joys.

⟜Minna Thomas Antrim,
1905

*H*e looked home-made, as though his wife had self-consciously knitted or somehow contrived a husband when she sat alone at night.

⟶Eudora Welty,
1941

My life is a bowl which is mine to brim
    With loveliness old and new.
So I fill its clay from stem to rim
With you, dear heart,
With you.

My life is a pool which can only hold
One star and a glimpse of blue.
But the blue and the little lamp of gold
Are you, dear heart,
Are you.

My life is a homing bird that flies
Through the starry dusk and dew
Home to the heaven of your true eyes,
Home, dear heart,
To you.

—May Riley Smith,
1936

Alexandra and Philip Yu, married for thirty years.

Oh, the comfort—the inexpressible comfort
  of feeling safe with a person,
Having neither to weigh thoughts,
Nor measure words—but pouring them
All right out—just as they are—chaff and
grain together—
Certain that a faithful hand will
Take and sift them—
Keep what is worth keeping—
And with the breath of kindness
Blow the rest away.

                    —Dinah Maria Mulock Craik,
                        1866

*S*ummer *is in* her face now,
and she skippeth.

— John Fletcher,
1621

The human heart, at whatever age,
opens only to the heart that opens in return.

> ⁓ Maria Edgeworth,
> 1814

Buster and Dorothy Williams, married more than sixty years
when this photograph was taken.

*H*e'd *nothing but* his violin,
  I'd nothing but my song;
But we were wed when skies were blue,
And summer days were long.

We sometimes supped on dew-berries,
Or slept among the hay,
But oft the farmers' wives at eve
Came out to hear us play;
The rare old songs, the dear old tunes,—
We could not starve for long
While my man had his violin,
And I my sweet love-song.

— Mary Kyle Dallas
(1830–1897)

I cannot say what loves have come and gone,
I only know that summer sang in me
A little while, that in me sings no more.

—Edna St. Vincent Millay,
1923

Writing on back of snapshot is faded, but note indicates
that this was taken in a "farm parlor."

A woman of 47 who has been married 27 years and has six children knows what love really is and once described it for me like this: "Love is what you have been through with somebody."

— James Thurber,
1960

good marriage is that in which each
appoints the other guardian of his solitude.

— Rainer Maria Rilke
(1875–1926)

*Winter visitors relax on the beach beside their car
near a trailer park in Sarasota, Florida, 1939.*

We are adhering to life now with our last muscle—the heart.

—Djuna Barnes,
1937

Photo: Dan Weiner

Acknowledgments

I have come to rely on my steady and supportive network of family, friends, and associates when any new book project gets underway. For this particular book, I'm particularly indebted to Jane Bergere, Sue Ellen Bridgers, Carolyn Bucha, John and Mary Louise Clark, Margie Haber, Ed Hernstadt, Patty and Bob Laufer, Erika and Gary Matt, Claire Whitcomb, and Karen Woodard.

Also, Joy Derr at Hood College, Terry Geesken at the Museum of Modern Art, Carol Hedges and Bob Krueger at Time Frame, Mary Motley Kalergis, Annamari Mikkola, John Mizon and Merrie London at Inspired Solutions, Barclay and Aggie Rives, Allen Rokach at *Southern Living,* Bernice Stewart, Leonore Simon, Cindy Sperling Spengler, Linda Wolcott-Moore, Cindy and Eddie Russell, Sandra Weiner, Buster and Dorothy Williams, and the staff at Archive Photos.

Once again, Gillian Speeth combed many archives with her fine sense of style; Leisa Crane brought to this second book her inestimable skills as a researcher, as well as her friendship and generosity. At Andrews McMeel, I wish to thank my editor, Christine Schillig, for her enduring support; Jean Zevnik and their skilled sales and marketing force; also my friend Carlie Collier for her wonderful hand-tinted photography for the jacket, and Virginia Norey for yet another splendid design.

On the home front, there's always my mother, Anita Kienzle, who's used to my many whimsical requests, my aunt Jerri Fowler whose timeless wedding photograph inspires everyone who sees it, and my smart sister, Jeanne Kienzle, for her words and for her constant support. As always, Ken was there, looking over my shoulder and saying just the right things.

Photo Credits

The following photographs, indicated by the page on which they appear, have been printed with permission: ii, 29, 33, 37, 56, and 63: Archive Photos; viii, x, 2, 44, 51, 64, 76, 82, 86, 91, 104, 116, and 119: Time Frame; xiv: photo by Allen Rokach, copyright Allen Rokach; 5, 92, and 128: courtesy Anita Kienzle; 13: courtesy Lenore Simon; 17 and 85: photos by Karen Woodard, courtesy

About the Author

*P*at Ross *(seen above with an early beau)* is the author of many popular books that relate to themes of home—specifically design, entertaining, and gardening—as well as titles dealing with women's issues, including *The Kinship of Women* for Andrews McMeel, and a humor book, *Menopause Madness.* Her lifestyle books include the best-selling *Formal Country, Please Come for Dinner,* and *Decorating Your Garden,* a Book-of-the-Month Club selection featuring three hundred of the author's own photographs. Pat Ross began collecting early photographs a number of years ago when she renewed a long-time interest in photography.

For many years, Pat Ross owned Sweet Nellie, a popular trendsetting Madison Avenue shop that specialized in American crafts and designs for the home. She now writes full-time from her home in New York City and a farm in McDowell, Virginia.